Sparkling Lights

Sparkling Lights

Live Boldy and Thrive

AD Krasikov

Copyright © 2025 AD Krasikov
All rights reserved.
ISBN-13: 979-8-9936073-0-6

No part of this publication may be reproduced, distributed, or transmitted in any form or by any means, including photocopying, recording, or other electronic or mechanical methods, or used in training of artificial intelligence (AI) or Large Language Models (LLMs) or by agentic artificial intelligence (AI) without the prior written permission of the publisher, except as permitted by U.S. copyright law.

For privacy reasons, some names, locations, and dates may have been changed. This publication is designed to provide accurate and authoritative information regarding the subject matter covered. It is sold with the understanding that neither the author nor the publisher is engaged in rendering legal or other professional services. While the publisher and author have used their best efforts in preparing this book, they make no representations or warranties with respect to the accuracy or completeness of the contents of this book and specifically disclaim any implied warranties of merchantability or fitness for a particular purpose. No warranty may be created or extended by sales representatives or written sales materials. The advice and strategies contained herein may not be suitable for your situation. You should consult with a professional when appropriate. Neither the publisher nor the author shall be liable for any loss of profit or any other commercial damages, including but not limited to special, incidental, consequential, personal, or other damages.

Book Cover created by using imagery from www.www.shutterstock.com, Illustration Contributor Bang_tomo, Illustration ID: 2628642765.
1st edition 2025

Dedicated to the person who thought they were not enough.

You were.

You are.

Contents

Acknowledgements i
Author's Note ii
Chapter 1 1
   Why are you here? 1
Chapter 2 4
   Who are you? 4
Chapter 3 13
   What do you want? 13
Chapter 4 17
   Where are you going? 17
Chapter 5 24
   Roadblocks, dead ends, and holes 24
Chapter 6 33
   Uncommunicated expectations are the recipe for failure. 33
Chapter 7 39
   Reality, networking, and self-promotion 39
Chapter 8 47
   It's not about you. 47
Chapter 9 52
   Imposter syndrome and faking it. 52
Chapter 10 59
   Moving on 59
Chapter 11 65
   Healing 65

Chapter 12	71
Thriving	71
Epilogue	74
Notes	78
About the Author	81

Acknowledgements

Thank you to the Sparkling Lights in my life that illuminated my path, paved the way, lifted me out of dark holes, and dusted me off when I fell.

Thank you to those who danced to their own rhythm, who showed kindness, gratitude, and love.

Thank you to those who encouraged me, and who helped me see my way through the darkness.

With each of you, you helped me reignite my spark. Helped my light to flicker, to flare, and finally to steadily blaze.

Author's Note

This is a book about life and the many lessons I have been through and the experiences that shaped me. I share it, not out of vanity or to glorify myself, humbly so that others may learn and scrape their knees a few less times or find themselves in less dark holes they have no idea how to climb out of.

This book is meant to entertain and enlighten. As a writer and a lover of words, I prefer my books to be pristine. The binding barely creased, where you cannot even tell I read them. The pages perfect, unmarked and without dog-ears.

If you are like me, it is okay. I give you permission to write in this book. Dog-ear your favorite pages. Make notes. Share what strikes you as worthy of sharing. Pass it around. Love it like your well-loved jeans until its edges fray and its binding loosens.

For it is my purpose to make a difference. In each life I am privileged to touch, I want to help your light shine, even if it fades in and out like a sparkling light.

As this book holds many of my experiences, I will change the names of those involved to protect their privacy. And, as in all things, there are always multiple sides to a story. This is my side, my perspective, and thus my reality.

Through my personal journey, mentoring prompts, and challenges may you find yourself and may you let your light brightly shine, without fear, without reservation and as your whole authentic self. Sparkling for all to see.

Chapter 1
Why are you here?

In life there are no right or wrong answers, there are only choices that lead to rewards or consequences.

- *AD Krasikov*

In these pages you will find examples and exercises to aid you with moving your life forward, and living as your whole and authentic self, joyfully and boldly.

As a multi-decade career veteran in financial services and a woman in the technology sector, I have often been asked to be a mentor and told I should author a book. Well, here we are. I will be honest, vulnerable, and open with you about my experiences.

If you think it is easy opening up about my pain, growth, and how I got where I am, please think again as it fills me with dread. But when I think about you, even though we have never met, and the chance that what I share may help you through what you are facing, I have no excuse.

I want you to get through the fire, up the hill, out of the hole, and to achieve your dreams.

I have chosen to draft this book as if I were speaking with you sitting across from me, and not blindly through these pages. It is my intent for it to feel more like a conversation than a lecture.

So, why are you here?

- Are you standing on the precipice of a decision, uncertain what to do?

- Do you not know where to begin, only that you are dissatisfied with where you are?

- Need a little boost, a swift kick in the hind parts, to get you back on track?

- Are you tired of the daily grind and feel like something is missing?

- Do you have a dream that you would love to achieve but it feels impossible?

Welcome! Together, we will help you:

- Understand who you are.
- Identify what you want.
- Develop and understand your purpose.
- Face your dream.
- Deal with roadblocks, dead ends, and deep dark holes.
- Understand how to set expectations and define success.
- Define reality, successfully network, and promote yourself.
- Discern when it is not about you.
- Recognize imposter syndrome and how to defeat it.
- Move on, and when it can be a good thing.
- And lastly, how to heal and thrive.

Before you start reading, quickly jot down a few outcomes you want to achieve by the end of the book:

_____
_____
_____
_____
_____
_____
_____
_____
_____
_____
_____

Understand that though I am sharing much of my personal journey as your mentor, this is about you. Your growth and your success. Be mindful and be honest with yourself.

This is not a time for judgement or self-criticism. It is an opportunity for reflection, for understanding who you truly are and stepping into your strengths, for unveiling your light and achieving more than you think, at this moment, you are capable of.

Chapter 2
Who are you?

Neither do men light a candle, and put it under a bushel, but on a candlestick; and it giveth light unto all that are in the house.

Bible, King James Version - Matthew 5:15

Each of us, though we live in societies and cultures that shape and mold us, are individuals. We each have our own value system, wants and needs, and personality. These affect how we understand and interact with the world around us.

At face value, the question "who are you?" may be effortless to answer. You spout your name, age, gender, whether you are married or a parent. But do these really answer the question of who you are?

To answer this question, I suggest you find a quiet spot and give yourself time to reflect.

The first time I answered it; I had about fifteen minutes. It was at a time management seminar. And the question was phrased not as "Who are you?" but as "What are the three most important things you spend time on in your day?"

You might ask, how are these the same questions?

The answer: The things you spend time on are the things you most value, which reflect who you are.

This is intensely personal. It is you.

This exercise comes with no judgement. You can choose to keep your answers private (or not). And you may want to give yourself more than fifteen minutes to put your answers together. Lastly, your answers are not final and may change.

I understand how difficult it is to narrow yourself down to just three words and three things you spend your time on. When I do this exercise, I think of these as defining words. They are aspects of myself without which I cannot thrive.

To help, let me give you an example:

I am…	I spend the Most Time Each Day On:
Creative	1. Faith
Honest	2. Family
Driven	3. Work

Let's break down the examples in my chart.

• Creativity is part of me. I have a vibrant and active imagination that spans this world and worlds of my own creation. To spend my days confined within a box of someone else's definition would cause me to wither.

• Honesty isn't the best policy, for me it is the only policy. I do not have the patience to lie and remember what I said to whom about what. Even if the truth is bitter.

This likely goes back to when I was a little kid in elementary school. I was in first or second grade and often stretched the truth. My cousins told me that if I lied the devil was going to come out from under my bed and take me. I stopped lying. Even when I got a waterbed.

• Being driven is not about ambition. It is about being better than I was the day before. This is a strength and a pitfall, because if I am not given expectations to exceed, I will set them myself and mine are always higher and harder to hit than what someone else gives me.

What about the things I spend my time on?

+ Sparkling Lights +

- My faith is at the top of my list because each day I am building and working on my relationship with God through Jesus. (This is my list, not yours. It is okay not to agree with me.)

- My family is next. I do what I do for them. I provide for them, support them, and want them to always be healthy, happy, and prospering. They are my lodestone.

- Lastly, work because it supports my family and enables me to do the things I want to do. Through it, I serve my purpose. We'll get to purpose later.

In the table below, choose three words that define you. Then, list the three "things" you spend the most time on in your day. "Things" is put in quotes because you get to define how high-level or detailed these items are in your list.

I am…	I spend the Most Time Each Day:
	1.
	2.
	3.

Now, it is time to really dig into who you are and who you choose to be. I did not say "want to be." I said "choose to be." **Each day, we make a choice about who we are and how we show up.** We either let it happen (default mode), or we make it happen (level-up mode).

I am an only child. My mom stayed at home until I started half-day kindergarten. She tried putting me in daycare, I hated it. I did not understand how to interact with other kids, I was more comfortable around adults – specifically, my mom. And, I had a physical disfigurement that gave kids an opening to tease and bully me.

When I was eight months old, I grabbed a freshly brewed steaming hot cup of coffee from the coffee table and tried to use it as leverage to stand. Instead, I dumped it all over my footie pajamas, which melted to me. The result was second- and third-degree burns on my right shoulder and arm, and on my neck and back.

Kids, if you do not know, are cruel. They find anything that makes a person different and use that against them. My burn scars were no exception.

What pieces of my personality may have developed because of these experiences?

- I am fiercely independent. (Only child.)
- I speak up and voice my opinions. (Adult conversation from an early age.)
- Fighter. (Will fight through adversity.)
- Introverted. (Learned early how to be alone. Besides being an only child, I was set apart because of my scars.)

From sixth grade through eighth grade, I attended five different schools. This gave me the opportunity to try out different personas and determine who I really was. By high school, I was ready to be me. Wholly and unapologetically me.

I learned:

- I like setting the bar and ruining the curve. (Highly competitive.)
- Sneaking out and breaking rules, not my thing. (Responsible.)
- I have traditional values. (Most people in high school do not.)
- Happiness comes from within. (Make yourself happy first and others will be happy with you.)

Even though these items comprise the distinct colors of glass in my stained-glass lenses, I choose which of them define me and where I spend, or give, my time.

In time management classes, you might be given the analogy of the glass jar. It goes something like this: you have big rocks, pebbles, and sand. You must fit all of it in the one jar. How do you do it?

If you put the sand and pebbles into the jar first, there is no room left for the big rocks. But if you put the big rocks in first, then the pebbles, and then the sand, it all fits.

What makes up the big rocks, the pebbles, and the sand is very personal and unique to each person. **We each get to determine what goes into our jar.** The jar is where you spend your time.

The big rocks in the jar are your top three things you spend your time on. For me, this is faith, family, and work. The pebbles are things like writing, reading, streaming, exercising. While the sand is made up of things like chores, eating, sleeping, and commuting.

Somedays, I have more pebbles than big rocks in my jar; and, somedays, I am raking a sand garden. On those days, when my jar is out of balance and there are rocks, pebbles, or sand sitting on the side, I must recognize that was my choice. Healthy or sick. Full of energy or drained of energy. It was my choice to fill the jar with what and how.

To learn about yourself and to intentionally decide who you are, ask yourself the following questions and record the answers.

- If you are not in the room, how do you want others to describe you?

  _____

  _____

  _____

- How do you think others describe you today?

  _____

  _____

  _____

- What are the gaps in how you want to be spoken of versus how you think people speak about you?

_____

_____

Let's talk about these three questions. How do you want others to describe you when you are not in the room? I want to be described as an honest, caring, intelligent and creative woman who inspires people to act, and who makes things happen.

How do you think others describe you today? AD is organized, charismatic, and a strong communicator. If you give her any assignment, she'll make it happen. Sometimes, she's a little pushy, too assertive (I've heard males call me aggressive), and takes on too much at once.

What are the gaps between these two statements:

My Perception	The Way I Think Others See Me	Gap Commentary
Honest	(Unknown)	Others assume people lie all the time.
Caring	(Unknown)	As an introvert, I am often seen as self-isolating, even though I deeply care about people and their needs.
Intelligent	(Unknown)	High intelligence can be off-putting.
Creative	Strong Communicator	Communicating isn't my only manifestation of creativity.
Inspirational	Charismatic	My desire to inspire can be viewed as charismatic, though I want to be inspirational.
Make things Happen	Pushy, Assertive, Aggressive, Intimidating	My workload level and what I can accomplish may not be the same as everyone else's.

Potential pitfalls to avoid based on how I want to be perceived:

- Sometimes, honesty is seen as too blunt and rude. I need to understand how to soften my words and phrase feedback in a positive way; and I need to reinforce with people that I will always be truthful with them.

- Though caring, I often look grumpy and do not hang out with people much. I need to let people know that when I am deep in thought, which happens often, my resting face is unfriendly. That does not mean I do not care, or I do not want you to talk with me. And if I am standing next to a wall in a crowded room, it is because I have a bit of "people-claustrophobia."

- I could speak like a normal person and not like a thesaurus. I need to consider my audience. Who am I meeting and communicating with? Should I use the standard sixth grade vocabulary or are these industry experts that expect a certain level of industry jargon?

- I have weird ideas, and lots of dragons. I boldly accept my weirdness and do not apologize for not thinking within any box. This means that some people may not accept or respect me.

- I have a lot of projects, activities, and ideas in the works. This means that I am often over-committed. I need to say "no" or "not right now" more often, and I need to delegate to keep all the flying monkeys in the air.

Now it is your turn to break down the two statements and identify gaps.

My Perception	The Way I Think Others See Me	Gap Commentary

What are the potential pitfalls based on your analysis that you should work on or accept?

_____

_____

_____

_____

_____

_____

You may have heard at some point in your life that perception is 100% a person's reality. That means how I perceive our interaction is my reality. How you perceive it is your reality. And, somewhere in the middle is the truth of reality.

✦ Sparkling Lights ✦

To check your perceptions, ask three to five (3 - 5) people how they would describe you, and where you excel and where they think you could improve. Offer to receive this feedback anonymously if they are uncomfortable. And do not just ask people who like you. Ask people who you have had challenging engagements with, as well.

With this information, check their feedback against what you wrote. Decide if you want to select any of their perceptions over your own and update the document. Remember, who you are is your choice, not anyone else's. Yours. **You cannot control how they perceive you, only how you react to it.**

Flash Points:

✦ This is intensely personal. It is you.

✦ Each day, we make a choice about who we are and how we show up.

✦ We each get to determine what goes into our jar.

✦ You cannot control how people perceive you; you can only control yourself.

Chapter 3
What do you want?

Let your light so shine before men, that they may see your good works, and glorify your Father which is in heaven.

Bible, King James Version - Matthew 5:16

This is not about wanting a vacation, a raise, a billion dollars, or a box of tacos. **This is about your purpose.** Your why. After all, we could all use a vacation, a raise, a billion dollars and a box of tacos.

What you want does not, and should not, have to be something material. It can be something inspirational, something that motivates you. This "want" is about the impact your life, your sparkling light, has on others and on this world that we cohabit.

Can what you want change as you, an individual, grow and encounter different experiences? Absolutely. Does it have to change? Not at all.

Let me give you an example about what I wanted in various stages of my life.

Stage 1	Stage 2	My Current Stage
I wanted to be remembered long after I died, like Shakespeare.	I wanted to advance in my career and support my family.	I want to make a difference.

If you consider the things I have wanted in my life, do they contradict each other? Or, over time, would you say I gained clarity?

- In stage one, I wanted to be remembered. As an only child, early in my life, I recognized that there would come a time when there was no one alive that knew me. This saddened me to think that one day, my light would be extinguished and forgotten, as if I never existed. I wanted to leave a lasting mark on the world and to be remembered. When you think of the "great" writers, they did just that. They created stories that resonate with people, which impart lessons and wisdom.

- In stage two, I became a wife and mother. My world became less about me and more about my immediate family. I poured myself into ensuring that they were supported, felt my love for them, and would flourish.

- In stage three, I realized that if I do not put some of my time and effort into myself that I would burn out and have nothing to give to my family. I did a lot of self-reflection and spent time thinking about what *I* really wanted. Yes, I wanted to be remembered. Yes, I wanted to provide for my family. These both boiled down to that I wanted to make a difference.

When I say these words aloud, "I want to make a difference," I feel them resonate inside of me. The vibration bounces off my ribcage like an echo bounces off rock. They are more than words. They are my purpose. My why.

Now, comes the hard part. What is your purpose, your why?

I am not pretending this is easy. This takes thought, deep thought and time with yourself. Really consider why you exist. Is it to irritate your sibling? Is it landing on Mars? Is it to bring happiness to others? Is it to help someone feel valued?

This is *yours*. Just like with the words that define you and where you spend your time, this is an exercise that is unique to you. Use the prompts below to iterate what you want until you create a one-line phrase.

Example: *I want to bring people to Jesus.*

I want...

I want...

I want...

I want...

I want...

From these statements, circle the two that you want the most. Then, see if you can condense them into one sentence.

For example: *I want to make a difference, and I want to bring people to Jesus.*

These are two stand-alone statements. As you review what you wrote, see if you can condense it even further to one easy-to-remember message.

For example: *I want to make a difference.*

Why do you think I removed the second part? No, not because it may offend someone. I did it because to me, if I am able to help someone build their relationship with Jesus, I am making a difference. The second part of the statement is included in the first part. I do not need to explicitly state it.

So – my want is to make a difference – I recognize that *how* I achieve my want can and will vary.

By understanding yourself and identifying your purpose, you will now be able to set your feet on a path.

Flash Points:

✦ This is about your purpose.

✦ Can what you want change as you, an individual, grow and encounter different experiences? Absolutely. Does it have to change? Not at all.

✦ How you achieve your purpose can and will vary.

Whereas ye know not what shall be on the morrow. For what is life? It is even a vapour, that appeareth for a little time, and then vanisheth away.

Bible, King James Version - James 4:14

Chapter 4
Where are you going?

So teach us to number our days, that we may apply our hearts unto wisdom.

Bible, King James Version - Psalms 90:12

If you are like me, you may dream about a road less traveled. A picturesque forest road with wildflowers lining its edges, trees that sway in the breeze and shade you from the sun, and a gentle but ever-increasing grade that eventually leads you to the top.

In that dream, I do not think about the challenges of this path. I do not imagine losing sight of the road due to overgrowth; or thunderstorms that roll over and douse me in freezing rain; or the dangers of wildlife that may be stalking me. I only see the positive, the beauty.

Reality though is messy. It is sweet and sour, easy, and hard. It isn't a static scene on a canvas. And, very rarely, is it ever a straight path.

If you were to open a map, electronic or paper, you would see a network of roads; many of which interconnect and intersect. Which do you choose for your route?

You choose the roads that will get you to where you are going based on your objectives, like shortest route, most scenic route, route with the most tourist attractions, or route with the most restaurants.

Wait – let's pause for a second and reconsider that last paragraph. "You choose the roads that will get you to where you are going based on your objectives." This assumes that you know where you want to go, and that you have objectives to meet along the way.

Do you know where you are going? Many people do not, so if you answered "No" you are not alone.

As kids, we are asked, "What do you want to be when you grow up?" As adults, we are asked, "Where do you see yourself in the next five years?" Both questions are equally difficult to answer.

As kids, we do not know all the possible jobs that exist which align with our interests. So, we gravitate to answers that are common like being a doctor, veterinarian, artist, race car driver, or fire fighter. I've never heard a child say prompt engineer, HVAC technician, forensic data investigator, or tactical weapons specialist.

As adults, have you ever heard someone say in the next five years, I am going to be a... travel writer, culinary entrepreneur, executive assistant, or in the same job I have now?

These questions are meant to inspire us but often all they do is demotivate us. We do not know what we do not know, and our dreams seem too far away to grasp, too unreal. After all, they are dreams.

I heard one of my boys' coaches challenge them by asking what their big hairy audacious goal was – that is to say, their dream. The boys started off at first giving small answers. The coach pushed them to think even bigger until their real dream materialized.

I am going to do the same for you.

What is your dream? My dream is to...

_____

_____

_____

Did you think big, or did you limit yourself?

Be truthful with the answer. Think without limits. What is your dream?

Let's talk through a few examples:

- My dream is to be a writer.
- My dream is to be a wildly successful writer.
- My dream is to be a wildly successful writer that inspires people through my writing.
- My dream is to be a wildly successful writer that inspires people through my writing, and that through my writing I can support my family and give back to my community.

What are the challenges with the above statements? Let's look at each of them.

- My dream is to be a writer.

Challenges: What kind of writer? A journalist, a novelist, a screenwriter, a cartoonist?

- My dream is to be a wildly successful writer.

Challenges: What defines success? Is it that I am published, earning an income, making a bestseller's list, or winning a contest?

- My dream is to be a wildly successful writer that inspires people through my writing.

Challenges: How will I know I have inspired anyone? I won't unless someone tells me I have. I can only assume that someone will be positively impacted by what I write. I can aspire to be inspirational, but I cannot really prove I am. So, this is more of a motivational statement than an action.

- My dream is to be a wildly successful writer that inspires people through my writing, and that through my writing I can support my family and give back to my community.

Challenges: This statement clarifies that success is not about money as the second part of it addresses wanting to support myself financially, but the vision is limiting.

Are any of these statements big, audacious, and hairy? Let me try again.

- My dream is to be a world-renown author with multiple best-sellers, series, and movie deals with stories and words that live beyond me to impact current and future generations.

Now, THAT is big hairy and audacious. Can you see the difference? Let's have you try again.

My dream is to…

_____

_____

_____

Just as we challenged my initial dream statement, challenge yours. Check that your dream is specific, that you will know when you have achieved it, that it scares you because that is when you know it is hairy and audacious.

Once you have defined your dream, make it into a goal. After all, dreams stay dreams while goals become achievements.

With your goal firmly in place, it is time to build out a plan. This may feel a bit overwhelming, that is okay. We are not trying to achieve the big hairy audacious goal all at once, but in pieces and over time. This is what creates your path.

A path is built by laying one brick in front of another or traveling the same way repeatedly until it is worn into the landscape. It does not happen overnight.

To achieve your big hairy audacious goal, break it down into smaller timebound and achievable goals. Remember, this is your dream, so your path (goals) may be different than the examples provided in this book; and your starting place may be different.

Big Hairy Audacious Goal: My dream is to be a world-renown author with multiple best-sellers, series, and movie deals with stories and words that live beyond me to impact current and future generations.

If I were to break this down into smaller goals, they may look something like this:

- Write one to four books every 12 months.
- Learn the business of writing within 3 years.
- Attend one writer's conference a year.
- Learn how to write a query letter.
- Learn how to connect with agents and editors.
- Learn about indie (or self) publishing.
- Learn about marketing and book promotion.
- Read books within my genres, at least three a year.
- Submit to agents one finished work each year.
- Publish, publish, publish – promote, promote, promote.

Each one of these goals should be refined to be specific, measurable, achievable, relevant, and timebound (SMART).

Admittedly, the challenge with being an author is that what you write must connect with an audience to be impactful; and it must connect with an agent or acquiring editor to be traditionally published. Any creative work is subjective. YOU must believe in it.

I started authoring short stories in elementary school and forayed into novel writing in high school. I shared my writing with my teachers and friends. By college, I was ready to bring my writing to the world and asked a trusted and respected professor to give me feedback.

He tore it apart. Crushed me.

The feedback he gave me, a budding and fledgling writer, was so strong that he set my goal back to the beginning. He made me question my very ability to write and tell a story. He made me not want to put anything I wrote in front of someone.

What I was not consciously aware of at that time was how very subjective the business of writing is. And, that audience is extremely important. Asking my Religious Studies professor to read a young adult fantasy romance fan fiction of Beauty and the Beast probably wasn't the right fit.

Then, life happened. I got married and had kids. I put my writing on the backburner to earn an income and take care of my family. The passion, the burning fire of creativity, inside me to share a rich internal life with the world yearned to be free – and, finally, I started writing again. A new book was born, and I shared it with a close friend of mine.

Unlike the professor, he told me that the story had potential but that I would benefit from joining a professional writing society and learning more about the business of writing, while also how to improve and mature my craft.

So, I did. I joined a local non-profit that supported writers and learned about the business of writing. I pitched the book I wrote and received professional feedback on how to make it better. Eleven years later, and nearly as many revisions, that story is ready to be published.

I am ready to move forward with the next step in my big hairy audacious goal. My path was not straight, and along the way, I learned about new objectives to help me reach my goal.

What are the smaller goals you need to achieve to reach your dream?

_____

_____

_____

_____

_____

_____

Next, number them and identify which you are going to do first and their sequential importance. Then, put realistic timeframes to accomplish them. Will it take a year to complete the first goal or 3 months? Do the same for each goal.

This is your path. Write it out on a piece of paper and tape it to your wall, your door, wherever you will see it. This is your commitment to yourself.

Flash Points:

✦ Your path must have a direction. This is your dream, which is your big hairy audacious goal.

✦ Dreams stay dreams while goals become achievements. Break your big goal into smaller achievable and timebound objectives.

✦ Check-in with yourself periodically to see if you need to adjust your goals and which ones you've completed.

✦ Be willing to pivot, life throws us curve balls all the time.

✦ You must believe in your goal, and in yourself. No one else's opinion matters. It is your goal, not theirs.

I can do all things through Christ which strengtheneth me.

Bible, King James Version - Philippians 4:13

Chapter 5
Roadblocks, dead ends, and holes

The righteous cry, and the Lord heareth, and deliverth them out of all their troubles.

Bible, King James Version - Psalms 24:17-20

I would like to tell you that once you know who you are, what you want, what your dream is and your path to get there that the rest is smooth sailing. Unfortunately, I cannot. People are unpredictable. Life is messy. Anxiety is like a flash freeze.

You will hit a roadblock or a dead end, and you will fall into one or more holes. It just is. What do you do though when it happens?

Advice I have received:

- Get a ladder and get over it.
- You need to rest.
- You are burning the candle at both ends, and in the middle, you are going to burn out.

None of the above was helpful.

You are the one who must decide if what you are working toward is worth it. Will it move your life forward? Does it tie directly to your purpose? Will it impact one or more of your goals? **If any of these answers are yes, do not give up! There is always a way.**

For roadblocks and dead ends, the way you bypass them is to broaden the box within which you are thinking. **Better yet, destroy the box. There is no box.** A box is a set of culturally defined, or personally defined, rules by which you are living.

Let's give an example.

When I was a first-year student in college, I worked at a retail store. On a Friday night, at 5 p.m., I was held at gunpoint and robbed. It was a surreal experience. My first thought when the assailant walked in and entered the turn style was, "Gee, that's a fake beard." I didn't have much time after that for any thoughts as he pulled the gun from under his brown leather bomber jacket and ordered me into the back room.

He stuck me in a bathroom and told me to stay there. I could hear him and his partner raiding the store. Then, a random ding as the front door opened. Soon after, a customer was herded into the bathroom with me. This happened several times. A few customers decided to try to stop the criminals. I stayed in the bathroom.

It wasn't long after that the customers were brought back into the small space, their personal belongings taken and their cheeks flushed, and clothes mussed. Thankfully, no one was hurt. When we could no longer hear any sounds from outside the bathroom, we ventured out to find the robbers gone. I called the police, called my manager, and closed the store.

After the police arrived and I gave my report, my manager told me to finish out my shift. They did not offer to stay with me, to ensure I was safe in any way. They just left. I was in shock. I was held at gunpoint. Threatened. Yet, I had to finish out my workday – by myself – and close out for the evening. It was time for a new job.

Finding part-time work as a college student, with limited work experience overall, was a challenge. I continued working at the retail store while applying elsewhere and eventually received an opportunity to interview at a computer store.

The manager of the store was willing to give me a chance, if I could prove that I could learn. He informed me that I would be tested as part of the interview process.

This is where the manager chose to think outside of the box. It was not important to him that I start the job *with* the knowledge. I had to prove to him I could *learn* from what he gave me and that I had the *initiative* to do so. So, he gave me the answers to the test.

Sometimes, what we think is a roadblock or a dead end is really our own construct. Morally and ethically, should he have given me the answers? No, he should not have. If what he wanted to know is whether I was coming to the job with existing experience. He already knew I didn't have the experience. So, what he wanted to know no longer fit in that box, and therefore neither did his solution.

Let me give you another example.

When I first started college, my major was either going to be archaeology or anthropology. I mean, who wouldn't want to adventure through the middle of the jungle and deep into hidden ruins. Or uncover history changing information hidden within the Dead Sea? Besides, the artifacts and ruins would fuel my imagination and storytelling.

Then, I participated in a historical archaeological dig in Southeast Colorado. Hot, dry, dusty, and boring. One meter by one-meter squares roped off into grids. Meticulously removing layers of dirt until a change in strata, or a rock, or something was found and then diagraming the changes. Taking what you removed and placing it through a giant sifting screen and picking through, piece by tiny piece. Only to find nothing. Repeat for hours on end.

I was relieved to be selected to go into the old cabin and slowly peel wallpaper from the walls so that I could uncover the layers and document the types. You read that right, peeling wallpaper off a wall layer by layer was more interesting.

Not to mention the spider bite that made me pass out and sent me to the doctor.

It was time to evaluate why I wanted to be an archaeologist. Really, I wanted to understand people. I wanted to study and observe, record, and author stories. This led me to changing my degree to cultural anthropology as my major, with a minor in organizational management. The minor was to appease my parents. They were not happy about me spending money on a degree they did not think would have a return on the investment. They wanted me to go into computers.

I thought that with this degree, I would be working my way towards becoming a museum curator. Instead, after working a few years, I shifted to using cultural anthropology and organizational management in the business world. Anthropology plays a key role in product development, design, research, and marketing.

In this example, the boxes were:

    1.   Degree field (major) – I spent many hours talking over college majors with my mom. We eventually landed on that I was paying for it, and I wanted to pay for something I would enjoy studying. Thinking outside of the box was to add the business minor.

    2.   Future potential – we do not know what the future holds. I could have picked a degree in computers and still not had career success. I broke the box on this one holding to what I was passionate about versus giving into the pressures of societal norms. (Side note, I ended up working on computers anyway!)

    3.   Reality check – going on an actual archaeological dig helped to break the romantic ideas created by the movie industry. This box was not only the bubble of my fantasy but also reframing what I wanted to achieve and do going forward.

What are some roadblocks or dead ends that you have encountered, and how did you overcome them?

Roadblock or Dead End	Box Buster

Now, on to deep dark holes.

These are not physical holes, but the emotional kind. The kind that makes your stomach sink, your heart race, and sleep a thing that other people do. They are often dug by anxiety.

If you are in a deep dark place, with no hope, and no one you can talk with – please, get help.

Understand, holes are dug over time. You can fall in small holes, the kind that makes you scrape a knee, like having a singular dreadful day at work. But the deep dark holes, you do not even know you are in until one day you realize you are stuck and cannot get out. Not because they just happened, but because you did not recognize the hole forming.

Let's say you are the sole provider for yourself or for your family. You have a lot of weight (responsibility) on your shoulders. The work you do provides food, shelter, transportation, and fulfills wants. Without your contribution, these items would dwindle and eventually cease to be.

Which makes risk-taking difficult. You want to pursue your goals. You want to fulfill your purpose. But you need to pay the bills.

These things need not be in conflict.

1. Know your purpose. Tie your purpose to your daily work. Answer for yourself, how your purpose and what you do to make a living work together. (This can help you get out of bed in the morning.) *If you cannot find a tie, then you may want to consider finding work that does fit your purpose.*

2. Take measured risks. Understand what could go wrong and what could go right if you take the risk. What can you do in advance to minimize things going wrong?

3. What can you do on the side to fulfill your purpose, if the day-job isn't cutting it? Consider turning a hobby into a side-gig or volunteering with a local non-profit that could use your skills.

If you have ever baked a loaf of bread, or watched it bake, there is a period where you let it rise. During this time, the bread is left covered in a warm moist place. The yeast in it feeds on the sugars in your recipe and the batter doubles in size.

This is like anxiety. It feeds on itself, and it doubles in size, repeating the process over and over again. What does this have to do with deep dark holes? I am getting to that.

As a project manager, I would organize and lead meetings. For these meetings, I would prepare an agenda, publish it in advance, organize any previous action items, prepare draft minutes, conduct and manage the meeting, asking clarifying questions throughout, and at the end I would pull together the final meeting minutes and publish them.

Sounds reasonable right? Except that I would be thinking about the meeting the evening before. Who would be in the meeting? What should I wear? What should I be careful about saying? Have I offended anyone in the meeting? Does anyone in the meeting have any current issues with anyone else?

Then, the meeting would happen. And I would spend the drive home and most of the evening thinking about that meeting and any other meetings I had. What did I say? Maybe I shouldn't have said what I said? Did I send out the minutes? What do I need to follow-up on? Did I interrupt anyone? What do I need to learn from?

It never stopped. Thoughts about work consumed me. The pit was being dug, and I was already sitting in it. My anxiety, and subsequent stress, never lessened and only grew.

I began praying for guidance. That's when I met a life-coach in training. She was (and is) a true blessing in my life.

The first request she made to me was to give myself permission, speaking aloud, to not think about work at a certain point in my commute; and to not think about work again the next morning until the same point in the commute.

So, I said: "I give myself permission to stop thinking about work on the way home when I reach the hospital." And "I give myself permission to think about work in the morning when I reach the hospital."

(The hospital was halfway between my house and the office.)

✦ Sparkling Lights ✦

This small thing was life changing. I admit, I had to say it aloud several times on different days, but it worked. It really worked. I stopped obsessing about work every single minute of my day.

Try it out:

I give myself permission to ... _____

_____

_____

_____

_____

But I was still in a deep dark hole. I was unhappy, anxious, and could not find a way out. Could I have talked to my family? Yes, but I did not want them to judge me. Could I have talked to people at work? Uh, maybe, but for other reasons I did not want them to judge me. Was my faith not strong enough? This had nothing to do with my faith in God. I know Jesus was with me. I did not have faith in myself.

I had lost my ability to love... me.

The next exercise my life coach had me do was to:

- Visually describe the hole I was in to her.
- Then, she had me think about someone I knew in my core who loved me and to describe that person to her.
- Next, she had me imagine that person reaching out to me in the hole and giving me their love to borrow until the day I no longer needed it.

Did this solve my problem? No, but it gave me the inner strength to do the things I needed to do to fill the hole.

What was necessary to fill the hole?

1. I had to remember my purpose.
2. I had to reconnect with my big hairy audacious goal – my dream.
3. I had to determine what I was spending my time on to rearrange my big rocks, my pebbles, and my sand.
4. I had to connect with myself and acknowledge my value and the things that "fill my bucket."

Things that fill your bucket are the things that bring you peace and joy. It is different for each of us. For me, being creative and whimsical fills my bucket. If I do not have time for these things, I start to shut down and have little to give to anyone else.

Think of it as a giant bucket full of water. Each time you do the things you need to do or help someone else by giving your time, you empty the bucket glass by glass. If all you do is empty the bucket, you will run out of water to give. That is the same here. You must find what fills your bucket and give yourself time to do these things.

It could be:

- Exercising
- Cleaning
- Crocheting or Knitting
- Reading or writing
- Gaming
- Larping (live action role-playing)
- Anything, really.

Whatever centers you, and bring you back to who you authentically are, can fill your bucket.

✦ Sparkling Lights ✦

Flash Points:

✦ Do not give up! There is always a way.

✦ Destroy the box. There is no box. A box is a set of culturally defined, or personally defined, rules by which you are living. So, stop trying to think inside the box.

✦ Know your purpose. Tie your purpose to your daily work. Answer for yourself, how they work together. (This can help you get out of bed in the morning.)

✦ Take measured risks. Understand what could go wrong and what could go right if you take the risk. What can you do in advance to minimize things going wrong?

✦ Find a side-gig that fulfills your purpose if the day-job isn't cutting it.

✦ Give yourself permission, aloud, to stop doing what is in your way.

✦ If you need to, borrow someone's love until you can love yourself again.

✦ Fill your bucket. If all you do is give, and never make time for yourself, you will be an empty husk in a deep dark hole.

For I am persuaded, that neither death, nor life, nor angels, nor principalities, nor powers, not things present, nor things to come, nor height, nor depth, nor any other creature, shall be able to separate us from the love of God, which is in Christ Jesus our Lord."

Bible, King James Version - Romans 3:38-39

Chapter 6
Uncommunicated expectations are the recipe for failure.

For with thee is the fountain of life: in thy light shall we see light.

Bible, King James Version - Psalms 36:9

Have you ever had someone ask you to clean the kitchen, which you do, and then they ask why you did not clean it?

These are uncommunicated expectations. Your understanding of a clean kitchen, your expectation of the work to be done, is different than that of the person making the request. Because the expectations were not discussed and agreed upon before the work was done, the work did not meet the expectations of the requestor.

You failed.

To ensure success, you must ask for clear expectations and ensure you understand them before undertaking a task. Sounds simple, it isn't always.

For example, a parent may not explain what a clean kitchen looks like to a child because they believe the child has lived in an example of a clean kitchen or has been part of cleaning a kitchen before. This puts the child in a bind. When they ask what the parent means by "clean the kitchen," they are often punished instead of given what the parent's expectations are.

If the parent were setting an expectation example, they would say something like, "I want the kitchen cleaned before I get home today at 6 p.m., that means I want: the dishes done, the trash taken out, the counters wiped down, the sink cleaned out, the floors swept and mopped, and the table cleaned off."

In the expectation example, the parent not only sets the expectations, they also ensure the child understands them. They ask the child to repeat the expectations in their own words so that they can agree upon them. And, if the child cannot, the parent can clarify anything that was not understood or not remembered. This ensures that the kitchen will be cleaned and there will be no timeouts or tears at the end of the day.

In the above example, the child knows exactly what the parent's expectations are. There is no room for interpretation or assumption.

As both workers and assigners of work, we need to be truly clear about understanding what someone wants accomplished and in giving details about what we want accomplished. This plays into every aspect of our life.

The entrance of thy words giveth light; it giveth understanding unto the simple.

Bible, King James Version - Psalms 119:130

At work, to be successful, we need to understand the expectations of our role. This is often described in a job description. If you do not have a copy of your job description, ask for one. Next, create a document for yourself about the expectations of your job and ensure you understand them. If you do not, schedule time to talk with your direct supervisor about the expectations so that there are no assumptions.

Not every job has a clearly defined set of expectations, some are more ambiguous than others. This means that if the person you work for cannot give you a clear definition of what they expect then you need to define for yourself what *you* expect. This has happened most frequently in my life when I have been part of creating a new department or role.

Sometimes, expectations are outlined in a performance review. These may be in the form of annual goals. Use this document as a tool with your supervisor so that you know what you are working toward each performance year.

Expectations are a success aid. By knowing what the definition of success looks like, you are more apt to achieve it.

Let's say you want to advance in your career at a specific company. You ask your manager what you need to do to be ready for the next promotion. Rather than answer you, your supervisor gives you a grid like this that lists the percentage of time spent for each grade of the job on specific work tasks.

Job Duties	Grade I	Grade II	Senior	Team Lead
Customer Service: sales and servicing	80%	70%	60%	30%
Inventory Management: product inventory, stocking, reordering		15%	20%	20%
Loss Mitigation: trend analysis, inventory placement, reporting, prosecution, and reclamations				20%
Training: completion of monthly training	20%	15%	10%	5%
Coaching: regular coaching of team members in policies, procedures, sales, and service.			10%	5%
Scheduling: scheduling of staff, on call for substitutions.				10%
Conflict Management: employee and customer escalations				10%

Was this table helpful for you in advancing your career? Yes. The manager is setting an expectation with you that if you can demonstrate that you are already doing the work of the level above you, that you will

✦ **Sparkling Lights** ✦

be able to advance. And, you know what you need to learn and work on to achieve the next level. The manager has put the expectation back on you to demonstrate initiative based on your expressed objective.

In our personal lives, it is important to recognize that if we do not give clear expectations that those close to us will try to meet them and may fail.

For example, you say that you want to have a date night. In your mind, you want a romantic outing with your partner where you are alone together, enjoying the blissful peace of each other's company. However, when the day arrives, you are surrounded by noise attending a local sporting event. It is a date night. You are together. But, not alone, and not in blissful peace.

The expectation of a date night was filled. The uncommunicated expectations of quiet, romantic, and alone were not met. This one is on you at that point, and it is a suitable time to own your own failure and not pin it on your partner. Just enjoy date night.

Let's take a minute to practice providing clear expectations.

You are asking for a new housecleaning service to clean your home. What are the expectations, or instructions, that you provide?

_____
_____
_____
_____
_____

Okay, step back a minute. Set the book down and take a sip of water, or your favorite beverage, then come back and re-read your expectations.

Are they clear? Do they:

- Define what success looks like?
- Define what "going above and beyond" looks like?

- What would raise your blood pressure if you came home and saw it was not completed? Was that on your list? Was it prioritized? What if they ran out of time before they got to it?

It can be difficult to define success. That's okay. The better you get at doing it, the more likely you are to achieve it.

So...

- What does success look like to you?
- What are your expectations for your life?
- What are your big rocks – yes, we are bringing these up again – and are they in your expectations? If they are not, why and are you prioritizing what matters to you?

Yes, achieving our big hairy audacious goal – our dream – is success. But that's big. It's hairy. It's audacious. It will take time to get there. We need incremental success, just as much as we need to see fireworks.

What are your daily expectations for yourself? For example:

- I expect to get up when my alarm goes off and not hit snooze.
- I expect to exercise for at least 15 minutes a day.
- I expect to tell my family I love them every day.

These are small accomplishable expectations. These work into the larger expectations, like:

- I expect to write in one of my books in process for at least 30 minutes every weekday.

Notice that these expectations are specific and timebound. They march me toward my goal. This is the same whether you are working on your personal goals or goals at work.

Take a few minutes and set up to five achievable daily expectations for yourself.

1. _____
2. _____
3. _____
4. _____
5. _____

Flash Points:

✦ Uncommunicated expectations are the recipe for failure.

✦ Expectations are a success aid. By knowing what the definition of success looks like, you are more apt to achieve it.

✦ Be specific, timebound, and clear when setting expectations.

✦ When someone asks you for clarification, they are not challenging you. They are trying to understand what you want so that they can make it happen.

And he shall be like a tree planted by the rivers of water, that bringeth forth his fruit in his season; his leaf also shall not wither; and whatsoever he doeth shall prosper.

Bible, King James Version - Psalms 1:3

Chapter 7
Reality, networking, and self-promotion

And the light shineth in darkness; and the darkness comprehended it not.

Bible, King James Version - John 1:5

Reality is "real," right? Maybe. We can agree that reality has tangible constructs which we have agreed upon names for – like table and tree – but our own biases and physical makeup can affect what we see and understand. If you are color blind, you may not be able to recognize green or red. That does not mean that green and red do not exist as colors, but it does mean that they do not exist as colors for you.

That is why I say that reality is not a fixed fact. It is based on perception. Your perception is your reality, and my perception is my reality. We make society work by agreeing upon a shared reality, and rules that govern that reality.

As such we must work within our own confines. Meaning, I work within my understanding of reality. If I want to share it with you, I must communicate it. I cannot make assumptions that your reality matches mine; unless the item we are discussing is within our shared sphere of cultural and linguistic understanding.

Like the example for table. In English, the word is table. In Spanish, the word is mesa. If I am an English speaker talking about the mesa (the flat mountain ahead of me), that may very well confuse the Spanish speaker who is thinking about the piece of furniture in the dining room.

Our reality is different.

Why does this matter? Because we must understand that we create a common and shared reality. **We cannot assume someone has the same shared experiences we do, and that they understand because we are using common language.**

Whether in your personal life or business, when you agree upon goals, objectives, and what success looks like ensure that you have a shared understanding of the words you are using.

And I do not just mean the big dictionary words or industry words that an outsider may not know. I mean familiar words like trust. If I say I trust you, do you know what I mean?

I may mean that I believe you will follow through on any commitments that you make, and you hold the same value system and sense of responsibility I do.

What you may understand is that I inherently believe you will be truthful and hold yourself to moral standards. There is nothing in your understanding about following through on your commitments. So, if you miss deadlines, you said you would make, have you broken my trust?

In your perception, the answer is no. In my perception, the answer is yes.

Another interesting point about reality is that you can only define your own. You can agree with others and create a shared reality, but you cannot accurately tell someone else what their reality is.

You can be in the same car with another person and have two different versions of what happened on the car ride. Each of you experience the world, the view, and the interruptions differently. These experiences frame your reality.

If I were to say that we had an enjoyable car ride, and you said we did not. Each could be right at the same time. I may want to know more and understand why yours was not enjoyable, but that doesn't mean either of our statements negates the other's.

The only person you have control over is yourself.

As someone who dwelled in a deep dark hole for quite a while, I learned that my inner monologue about the thoughts and feelings of other people was all fiction. It was blatantly incorrect. Even if it wasn't, it was a construct of my own making. I never asked the people I was creating thoughts and feelings for if I was right, I just assumed I was. This caused my anxiety to spike, and feelings of self-doubt and negativity to flourish.

I had to "**stop writing other people's stories**" and focus on my own.

Remember how I shared that I would obsess about work? Well, part of that obsession was me writing other people's stories. Unless someone directly tells you what they are thinking, you do not know. Even if their body language is saying they disagree with you, it just may be that they have indigestion and are trying hard not to pass gas. Do not make assumptions. You do not know.

And, if you are good at creating someone else's internal monologue, it can be exceedingly difficult to stop doing it. This takes time, and a whole lot of reminding.

The only story you can write is your own.

As someone who loved to be the center of attention, again only-child; it was very out of character for me to draw inward and to stop gleefully approaching people I did not know.

In my childhood, I was fearless.

At three, while in my parents' gas station, I would approach customers for pennies to buy gum. And, cheeks bulging like a chipmunk, I would receive those pennies.

My parents called me the bathroom monitor because it did not matter what restaurant we went to, I had to check out the bathroom. Invariably, I made friends along the way and would have random people waving goodbye to me as we finished our meal and left.

✦ Sparkling Lights ✦

And, if there was an elevated fireplace hearth, it was a stage. I would get up and dance. It did not matter if the fireplace was at home or the local pizza place. It was my stage.

Fast-forward to adulthood and my professional life, by ten years I was starting to withdraw. I was encouraged to not be so bold, to appreciate and respect the hierarchy, to anticipate a lack of respect by my peers and management, to cater to other people and not myself.

My light dimmed, and rather than sparkle, it began to timidly blink. Many times, rather than shine, I would purposefully drape something over my light; because it was riskier for people to see it than it was to hide it.

It was at this point my life coach appeared. Not only did she help me love myself again, and to understand my priorities and dreams, she helped me reconnect with who I authentically am.

The first small step was to learn how to network. Having withdrawn and pulled away from people, it was intimidating and panic-inducing to attend a work event. The thought of putting myself out in public and being forced to make small talk was too much to bear.

Her solution was to think about questions I could ask other people. **People like to talk about themselves, if you give them the chance**; and this meant I did not have to talk about me.

Let's imagine you are attending a company training with industry professionals like yourself, who come from various parts of the country. You might ask:

- Where are you from? How was your trip?
- Tell me about your company.
- Tell me about your role, I have not heard of that position before.
- What challenges are you, or your department, facing in the next year?
- What projects are you currently working on?

These types of questions open the door for conversation and help you get to know the person, allowing you to think about other questions to ask or potentially to open up about yourself and what you, or your team, are working on.

Networking is about:

- Getting to know people.
- Understanding how you can help them, and how they could potentially help you.
- Gathering contact information to follow-up after the event, should you want to.

It is not as hard or as terrible as you might think.

- Stick to writing your own story.
- Be curious about other people.
- Be willing to be appropriately open about yourself.

You are a brilliant, shining light, sparkling for the world to see. You are unique. There is no one in this world, not even your twin, who is exactly like you. One of the best gifts you can give to the world is to be wholly and authentically yourself.

Some of us are good at self-promotion. Others feel like it is bragging and find it embarrassing. We wait for a superior or a peer to recognize us and call out what we have done. And… we wait, and wait, until the time passes and the opportunity for recognition fades.

If we do not tell people what we have accomplished, they will never know. There are times in life where promoting yourself is necessary.

I am not saying be self-absorbed. I had a previous coworker who shamelessly plugged himself, even setting his test password as "BobsaStud." It worked for him though. People laughed about it and his own confidence had people sighing over him like a high-school crush.

But that kind of arrogance is not for me. I am more reserved, and I find self-promotion difficult. I find it embarrassing. It is something that I must make myself do.

To promote yourself, you must know what you have achieved.

- Keep a record of your achievements, personal and professional.
- Add achievements to your resume and professional profile.

- When completing documents like an annual performance review, add the achievements from that year into your review.
- If your achievements are connected to your big hairy audacious goal (your dream), use them when promoting your dream to yourself and to others.

Examples of potential self-promotion with metrics:

- Saved over $100,000 through an efficiency project.
- Launched a digital platform used by more than 150,000 people.

Example of self-promotion, without metrics:

- I am a writer. I write technical documentation, fantasy, speculative fiction, and non-fiction.

Today, where we are surrounded by content, it is important to highlight our achievements and progress.

A few years ago, my mom reminded me that when I was in middle school, I saved a girl from drowning. Until she recounted the story for me, I did not even remember it happened. Not because it was not a significant event in my life, but because I believed that anyone in my situation would have done the same. For me, it was normal and not an extraordinary achievement. However, for my mom, it was a highlight in my young life.

I share this because I want you to think through what you deem ordinary, something anyone would do, and question yourself if that is really true.

For me, being part of a large project to launch a new software program is normal. It is part of my everyday life. That is not the same for most people. Being part of a team that launches software that will improve the lives of one hundred thousand people is noteworthy. It is worth promoting what part you played in the process and the impact it had on others.

Take a few minutes and jot down a few examples in your life that should be promoted, or that you thought were normal but maybe were not.

Things you thought ordinary that were extraordinary:

_____
_____
_____
_____
_____
_____

Projects, presentations, work assignments or volunteer assignments that you led or participated in that had a big impact on a company, a team, a group of people, or an efficiency ratio, profit ratio, etc.

_____
_____
_____
_____
_____

Consider which of these examples may need to be added to your resume, and expanded on with relevant details, to aid in promoting yourself.

Though self-promotion is often uncomfortable, it is necessary. If you do not share what work you have been part of, no one will no what you are capable of.

Do not hide your sparkling light under the blanket of someone else's reality. Share it with others and light the darkness for yourself and those around you.

Flash Points:

✦ Your perception is your reality, and my perception is my reality.

✦ We cannot assume someone has the same shared experiences we do, and that they understand because we are using common language.

✦ The only person you have control over is yourself.

✦ Stop writing other people's stories. The only story you can write is your own.

✦ People like to talk about themselves if you give them the chance.

✦ Networking is not as hard or as terrible as you might think.
- Stick to writing your own story.
- Be curious about other people.
- Be willing to be appropriately open about yourself.

★ If we do not tell people what we have accomplished, they will never know.

Henceforth I call you not servants; for the servant knoweth not what his lord doeth: but I have called you friends; for all things that I have heard of my Father I have made known unto you.

Bible, King James Version - John 15:15

Chapter 8
It's not about you.

Woe unto them that call evil good, and good evil; that put darkness for light, and light for darkness; that put bitter for sweet, and sweet for bitter!

Bible, King James Version - Isaiah 5:20

This entire book, until now, has been about you. Who you are. What you want. Your purpose. Your dream. Your path. Now, I am saying "it is not about you."

This pertains to other people's emotions and actions. **You can only control yourself.** Most of my life, I have deeply felt other people's emotions and took responsibility for those emotions.

It was not until I was working with a cognitive behavioral therapist that I had the following revelation:

- Someone else's emotion is theirs. You do not have to accept it.

What?!

In my young life, my father was an alcoholic. He would come home drunk, calling me all sorts of names, and many times would get into a verbal argument with my mom. I did not understand what he was going through or why he was angry. At that time, I had no idea it had anything to do with PTSD from Vietnam. I just knew he was mad, so someone had to be to blame. Whether it was him, my mom, or me.

✦ Sparkling Lights ✦

I wish I knew then what I know now. His anger belonged to him. It did not belong to me, or my mom. Neither of us had to accept it.

Whether someone is angry, depressed, stressed, or whatever emotion they are feeling, you have a choice to accept that emotion into yourself and feel it or to acknowledge it and that it is theirs. Just because someone is mad does not mean you have to be mad. You can accept that they are angry and determine why they are angry and address the issue that made them angry versus taking that emotion into yourself or owning that emotion as your own.

At work, the scenario can be a little less obvious.

I once attended a project meeting that was called by one of the top executives of the company. It was to address a project that was way behind schedule and over budget. The conference room had a typical layout, rectangular with a long table and chairs. The project team, which included top executives and business leaders, all filed-in at the appointed time. Right on the hour, the executive entered and sat at the head of the table. His body language said it all. This was not going to be a good meeting.

Immediately, he addressed the issue and calmly explained that the project would wrap up by a specific date – no ifs, ands or buts. Missing the date would not be tolerated. Jobs were threatened. In this same meeting, he removed the incumbent project manager and gave me the project to lead.

The project team might have felt:

- Threatened
- Hurt
- Lack of trust
- Incompetent

Instead, the team chose to see this as an opportunity to buckle down and prove they could make it happen. Rather than being demotivated by feelings of inadequacy and the threat of job loss, they found ways to motivate themselves to accomplish the task.

In short, they accepted the message and took accountability for their previous mistakes and not the emotions the message evoked.

When I was a director at a company, a peer female and I were brought into a conference room by one of the chief executives. Both of us had been with the organization for more than ten years and had worked collaboratively throughout the organization.

We knew how to effectively interact with peers and leaders. The chief sat down, crossed one leg over the other in an open stance, leaned back, and rested his hands behind his head. (If you do not know, this is a classic non-verbal power position.)

Neither my peer nor I knew why we were brought into the conference room. We had been given no reason for the impromptu meeting. He then proceeded to scold both of us on our behavior, which included interrupting people in meetings. When he concluded and left, both of us were stunned.

As long-time leaders in the organization, we had never been treated so poorly, received such criticism (which he treated as feedback), nor been told to sit down and shut up though in more polite terms. Let me tell you the emotions this interaction fueled:

- Self-doubt
- Inadequacy
- Lack of trust
- Lack of motivation

I went back to my previous performance evaluations to see if anything he said was ever documented. It was not. There was no secondary validation of his opinions. The more I thought about it, I wondered why we both were brought in to face his criticisms at the same time.

When I was hired, I was one of three females in the Information Technology department. We were all about the same age and blond. Throughout my career, I was often mistaken for one of the three even though we moved into different departments and roles.

My peer, who experienced the odd meeting with me, was also female, of a similar age, and blond. All I could think of is that wherever this feedback came from, the chief executive did not know which female it applied to (if it really applied to either of us) so he brought us both in to upbraid.

In my next one-on-one with my manager, I shared what happened and requested her input. She agreed that the meeting was not kosher and that she never experienced any of the behavioral traits called out. Though, to mind the peace, she encouraged me to "wait to speak" in future meetings. This just meant letting the male executives in positions higher than mine speak first.

Initially, I accepted that in some way I was wrong. As a leader in the organization, the executive would not just pull us aside unless there was some truth in it.

So, I became "lesser." I dimmed my light, was slower in giving my opinion or sharing an opinion at all. The ripple on the pond I made became almost non-existent. Except, this was *his* truth. Not mine.

When I realized that all the negativity around me was *their* truth, it allowed me to begin choosing what I accepted and did not accept.

My light began to brighten. I realized that:

- I provide thoughtful and strategic insights that are relevant.
- I am more than adequate. I have strong and valuable skills. This threatens people who are not as bold as I am.
- I do not need to be who *they* want me to be; I need to be who *I* want to be.

I do not have to accept someone else's reality of me. Their reality and their emotions belong to them, not me. What a freeing moment!

The moment you choose to step into who you wholly and authentically are your life takes on new vibrancy, joy, and fullness.

I did not have to accept their feedback or their emotions. It was for me to choose what to take in, learn from, and use.

This does not come easy. Practice and execution are difficult. If you keep at it, these are skills that will become part of who you are.

Flash Points:

✦ You can only control yourself.

✦ Emotions belong to the person having them. You do not have to accept someone else's emotion (or reality) and take it into yourself. Instead, you get to choose.

✦ You have your emotions; they do not have you.

✦ You own your reality. Do not accept someone else's version of you.

✦ Be wholly and authentically you. No one will ever light up a room the way you do. Your sparkling light is unique and has value.

Beloved, I wish above all things that thou mayest prosper and be in health, even as thy soul prospereth.

Bible, King James Version - 3 John 1:2

Chapter 9
Imposter syndrome and faking it.

What time I am afraid, I will trust in thee.

Bible, King James Version - Psalms 56:3

Have you ever looked in the mirror and wondered if it was really you looking back? Have you felt uncomfortable in your skin, with what you were wearing, the job you were performing, or with the conversation you were having?

You might have experienced imposter syndrome. This is when you feel like an imposter, even when you are not. It can be a crippling experience, and it can happen at any point and in any scenario in your life.

I had the opportunity to interview a top editor at a large publishing house, who had been in the industry for almost thirty years. She shared that even with her tenure and as a leading person in her field – she still felt like an imposter.

No one – not even one of us – can know everything. Every single one of us is fallible. We will make mistakes. And do you know what? That is okay.

We all must start somewhere, and we grow along the way.

As an author, I was reticent to share that I write and what I write because I was not published. I did not think anyone would take me seriously. Did it mean I was not an author because I was not published? No. But, it felt that way. I felt like an imposter.

If my dream is to be a world-renown author with multiple best-sellers, series, and movie deals with stories and words that live beyond me to impact current and future generations, then I need to live this dream.

To live the dream, I need to act on my plan to make it happen. That means I need to accept that I am an author and that I am taking steps, no matter how small, towards that dream.

If I continue to accept that I am an imposter, pretending to be an author, my dream will never be realized. It will sit on the shelf, gathering dust.

To conquer your big hairy audacious goal, you must be bold. To be bold, you must accept that there are times you will be uncomfortable, even in your own skin, and that is okay – it is really you, and not an imposter.

This is usually about the time that someone in your life will give you the advice to "fake it until you make it." They are not saying to update your resume with creative license. Your job at a local fast-food place is not the same as a sous chef at a five-star restaurant.

What they are saying is for you to assume the characterizations of someone who has already achieved your goal.

- If you want to be a manager, act like a manager.
- Dress like the managers in your company or the company where you want to work.
- Observe how they speak and act, and model that behavior.

For example, when I first started in financial services it was a very traditional industry. Bankers wore black or dark-blue suits, the men in coats and ties, and the women in skirts and heels. Pantyhose was a requirement.

At my first interview, I dressed in a navy-blue suit with a knee-length skirt. My hair was cleanly tied into a French twist. My nails were clipped and shining. My shoes were polished. My jewelry was classy – just a hint of gold, with a chain and small earrings. Mind you, I was applying for a job in Information Technology. A field where people often crawled under desks and installed cables, but that didn't matter. The job was at a credit union.

I dressed in the way I saw professionals in financial services dress. I looked the part. I looked like them, even though I had never worked in banking before.

This is important. People, subconsciously and without intentional bias, often select other people who look, act, and sound like them. Dressing the part is a critical piece of a job interview. If you normally have brightly colored, or multi-hued hair, multiple piercings, visible tattoos, or gauges – does your personal appearance reflect the brand of the organization, or the job, you are attempting to join?

This is where "fake it until you make it" comes into play. You need to modify your personal appearance to reflect the industry or organization you are trying to become part of. Unless, of course, you work for yourself.

Wait, wait, wait. In the last chapter, I said to be wholly and authentically you. Why now are we having to hide our light to be accepted? Straight-forward answer. Because the world is not fair.

Difficult answer. Do not hide your light. Just because you are updating your appearance, speech, et cetera does not mean you cannot keep who you authentically are in the process.

During another interview, still for a job in financial services, I chose to be wholly and authentically me. I still dressed appropriately. I wore nice black slacks, a black blazer, and a blue tank top. My hair was down, long, and straight. My earrings were modest hoops. I dressed in the way I thought a modern executive would dress.

And, during the interview, I chose to answer the questions as my full and authentic self. Not as who I thought they wanted me to be. But, as me. This means I showed them my humor. I shared that I am a writer, right off the bat. I let them know that I am creative and ambitious. I even shared about my resting b!tch face (RBF). And I did not curse, so it was difficult to do.

It was my choice to connect with this group of interviewers as me. It let me step into the role as my whole self, right from the start. No hiding. No facades. No faking it. Just me. Boldly and audaciously me.

If I got the job, which I did, it set the stage for me to live as who I am and not as who I think I *should* be to fit the role.

As you think about your dream, and what you want to accomplish in your life, where are you feeling like an imposter?

_____
_____
_____
_____
_____

What are you "faking" until you make it?

_____
_____
_____
_____

Let's talk a little bit about branding and what it means to create a personal brand.

A brand is often conceived of as a logo and a name. That is part of a brand, but not the whole brand. A brand is a living, breathing, growing concept that is comprised of imagery, tangible items, values, and culture which evokes a connection, often signified by feelings within a consumer.

Think about it like this, when you think of a luxury car brand – any one of them – you imagine what the interior of the car feels like, smells like, what the outside looks like, how it drives, and the level of support you expect from the manufacturer in caring for the vehicle. This is the brand of the automobile. It is consistent. You know what to expect and whether you want to align yourself with the vehicle by purchasing and driving it.

Another brand might be a fast-food restaurant that only serves chicken. They are closed one day out of the week, so that their employees can worship and be with family. Employees are always positive, polite, and the food is consistently good. You know what to expect. You do not go there with the intention of getting a hamburger or eating vegan. They serve chicken.

A person's brand is similar. It is made up of who you present yourself to be, what you say and do, and how you consistently "show up."

To make this more concrete, let us examine a few examples:

- Jen is a caring, thoughtful person who always remembers everyone's birthday, surprises others with small gifts, and completes her work on time though there may be a few small errors, like typos in her messages. She has an athletic build, wears her shoulder length hair in a ponytail, and likes to dress in comfortable but casual business clothing.

- David always shows up with a smile, lightens the moment with humor, and tends to be late turning in his work and may miss deadlines. He has an average build, likes to wear jeans and T-shirts when he can, but will wear the occasional polo. He can often be found chatting in someone's office, the hallway, or the break room.

- Tamera is diligent about deadlines, finds all errors in documents and in work processes. Her unnaturally colored pink hair is cropped short, her word choices would embarrass a seasoned Navy veteran, and she has little tolerance for excuses. She sometimes wears business professional outfits, and sometimes very casual home-appropriate outfits to the office.

What can we expect of each person based on their brands?

	Jen	David	Tamera
Brand Description	Team Mom	Relax, live a little	Life is short
Expectations	On time, easy-going, goal-setter, family-oriented, team morale is important.	Will be late, needs deadlines and oversight, will keep activities fun.	Expect the unexpected, deadlines to be met, and that others' opinions may not carry much value.

If you want to be considered for a role, and your brand does not fit that role, what might you need to do?

- Observe people in the role you want and their personal brands.
- Decide what changes to your brand you want to make, that are still authentically you.
- Change your behavior, dress, and attitude to reflect the new brand and consistently model it. (In other words, fake it until you make it.)

No one starts life, a new career, or even home repairs as an expert. To become experts, we must learn, try, fail, and try again. Be curious, be bold, be thoughtful. The only imposter in the room is the one sitting on your shoulder whispering lies that you aren't good enough.

You've got this.

Flash Points:

✦ We all must start somewhere, and we grow along the way.

✦ Accept that there are times you will be uncomfortable, even in your own skin, and that is okay – it is really you, and not an imposter.

✦ People, subconsciously and without intentional bias, often select other people who look, act, and sound like them.

✦ Just because you are updating your appearance, speech, etc. does not mean you cannot keep who you authentically are in the process.

✦ Your personal brand is made up of who you present yourself to be, what you say and do, and how you consistently "show up."

In the morning sow thy seed, and in the evening withhold not thy hand; for thou knowest not whether shall prosper, either this or that, or whether they both shall be alike good.

Bible, King James Version - Ecclesiastes 11:6

Chapter 10
Moving on

He that covereth his sins shall not prosper: but whoso confesseth and forsaketh them shall have mercy.

Bible, King James Version - *Proverbs 28:13*

In my undergraduate studies, I took a course titled "Death and Dying." Remember, I am an anthropologist by degree. It was a fascinating course, as we learned about, discussed, and sought to understand the way diverse cultures internalize and manage death.

There is, of course, the normal process of death that we all think about – which involves the end of a person on this earth. Many cultures fear that the deceased will return to haunt them, possess them, or curse them; others celebrate the deceased, knowing they have moved to the afterlife.

But, moving on does not have to be only the death of self here on earth. It is also moving on from one job to another, from high school or university, from a relationship, or a project. It can even be from one version of yourself to another.

When we move on, we must declare an end. For a new job, it is the last day of the old job. For high school or university, it is the day of graduation. For a relationship, it is the day of the break-up. For a project, it is the day the project is complete (like your walls painted or a book launched).

It is a little harder to identify when we have moved from one version of ourselves to another. There is not a clear line, a hard date, or a true stop. It is often a gradual progression, like a butterfly forming a chrysalis. It takes time.

Give yourself grace, you may not see the transformation while it is happening.

My own chrysalis was made not of silk but digital papyrus. My first finished book, a retelling of a story I created years before, received encouraging but unfavorable feedback. It was not what I hoped for. I wanted to hear praise. Instead, I heard encouragement and received advice on learning the business of writing.

That led to almost ten years of learning the business while continuing to write, and re-write, that one story. I wrote others, as well, but nothing felt ready for public consumption. Until, one day, at a hair salon while I was getting highlights added to my hair, I asked my stylist if I could read her some of the book I was writing.

She said yes, and I started reading aloud. It was her, another stylist, and two ladies in the building. I did not realize that by the second chapter, everyone had fallen silent. They were all listening. When my appointment was finished and I stopped, the ladies asked me where they could buy the book.

Elated, and chagrined, I shared that I was writing it and that it was not available yet. This one act of courage, on my part to read the work aloud, and their interest, bolstered me to continue writing despite the challenges.

Writing is an extremely subjective business, and not everyone will enjoy nor find the work you create worthwhile. That is okay. I had to learn this. It helped me move from feeling like an imposter to embracing myself as a writer.

Yet, in my day job, life was getting more difficult. I was feeling marginalized, suppressed, and thwarted. My stress was rising. Anxiety was my constant and unwanted companion. It got so bad that at one point after a small error, I climbed under my desk and cried.

You read that correctly. I was so overwhelmed, stressed, anxious, and burned out – expecting to be reprimanded and let go at every turn – that I hid under my desk and cried.

I recognized at that point that it was time to move on. This was not a stress-free recognition. Remember, these realities were not built all at once. They were built insidiously over time. My light had dimmed, my brand was battered, my purpose diminished – by multiple events and interactions over years.

Before I could move on, I had to identify what I wanted.

- What was I looking for in a new role?
- What would excite me to do, day-in and day-out?
- How much was I willing to disrupt my life and the lives of my family?
- What did I want to see in a new company that was different from my existing company?
- How important was aligning my purpose with the role?

Once I had answers to these questions, I not only looked for new opportunities that fit my criteria, but I also prayed. I got down on my knees and prayed.

But the LORD is with me as a mighty terrible one: therefore my persecutors shall stumble, and they shall not prevail: they shall be greatly ashamed; for they shall not prosper: their everlasting confusion shall never be forgotten.

Bible, King James Version - Jeremiah 20:11

I learned during this process that in the world of hiring and recruiting, tenure is seen as a negative. Recruiters and companies expect a person to have a new job, at a new company, every three to five years. If you do not, they want to understand what is wrong with you, and not why you stayed. It helped that I was able to explain, that though I was with the same company for a long time, that I had moved roles and learned new things every three- to five-years.

✦ Sparkling Lights ✦

Moving on takes courage. You must:

- Know who you are.
- Know what you want.
- Understand how to promote yourself.
- And actually, promote yourself, talk about yourself and the things you do well.

It takes action.

Inaction is comfortable. An object at rest stays at rest. An object in motion stays in motion. If you are comfortable where you are, you will not move on. You must make yourself take the necessary action.

That is probably one of the reasons you are reading this book. There is something in your life that you are dissatisfied with or you want to improve. No one can make it happen, except you.

No one can:

- Lose weight for you.
- Achieve your goal(s) for you.
- Be who you are meant to be.

What do you want to stop doing or move on from?

_____
_____
_____
_____

What is preventing you from moving on?

_____
_____
_____
_____

Read the items you listed. Honestly, and without bias, see if the reasons boil down to fear.

Fear is a true limiting factor. We fear both failure and success. But we should not let it control us. Fear should never be a reason for not doing something. You can be afraid and still take the leap.

I was given the opportunity to relocate from Colorado to Texas. If I were the only one to consider, it would have been an uncomplicated decision. But I wasn't. I needed to consider my immediate and extended family. The move would include me, my husband, and two of our four children. This meant that I was not only relocating but geographically dividing my family.

It tore my heart to leave two of my children behind, but I knew they would be supported by their grandparents and that they were at the age of adulthood. At any time, they could have chosen to move away. I was just hastening the event.

Still, with the two in high school, I needed to consider what the change would mean for them. What kind of environment they would be moving into, and what effect it might have on them. In the end, though we did reference calls, talked with friends and friends of friends who lived in Texas, we still had to just take the leap.

It all worked out. I took a fulfilling position and my family flourished.

We cannot let fear prevent us from living our lives. In life, you must make decisions. These decisions, or choices, may be given value statements of right and wrong. "That was the wrong choice." Or "That was a stupid decision."

This is an incorrect way of looking at life choices. With life choices, there are no right or wrong answers. There are only consequences and rewards. A choice could lead to negative consequences like losing your job or a reward like being promoted. As adults, we learn to anticipate and live with the consequences and appreciate the rewards.

If a decision did not turn out the way you had hoped, learn from it and move on.

Flash Points:

✦ When we move on, we must declare an end.

✦ Give yourself grace, you may not see your transformation while it is happening.

✦ Moving on takes courage.

✦ Moving on requires action.

✦ No one can move on, or forward, for you.

✦ Moving on is scary and uncomfortable.

And we know that all things work together for good to them that love God, to them who are the called according to his purpose.

Bible, King James Version - Romans 8:28

Chapter 11
Healing

Not that I speak in respect of want: for I have learned, in whatsoever state I am in, therewith to be content.

Bible, King James Version - Philippians 4:11

I am certain that you have heard "nobody's perfect." That is correct. Not one of us is perfect. Every one of us will make mistakes, hurt someone we do not mean to hurt, fall, and fail.

It is okay.

Get out from under the desk, wipe your eyes, and take a deep breath. You are okay.

In sports, I have heard the word "fail" broken down to "First Attempt in Learning." Failure is a step towards success. From each failure we learn a little more about ourselves, about the process, or the activity. When we apply what we learn, we get better. That means, the next time, we may not fail. We may even succeed.

Through this process, **it is important to give yourself grace and forgiveness.**

We are likely to forgive someone else, but less likely to forgive ourselves. We often beat ourselves up, verbally if not physically, over failures. Don't. Words matter.

Rather than call yourself an "idiot" or say something like "that was stupid," try "that hurt" or "let's not do that again." Admittedly, you may not be the one that is demeaning you or negatively correcting your failure. Instead, you may be the recipient of someone else's opinion.

You get to choose what you accept and what you do not. Another person's opinion is their reality; it does not have to become yours.

To forgive is difficult. Forgiveness means holding no ill will towards yourself, or someone, over a failure or a "wrong" done to you. It means letting go. Not thinking about it. Not dwelling on it. Not seeking revenge or recompense. It is over.

When you make a mistake, learn from it and move on.

To heal, you must forgive.

In life, our wounds are not always visible. I have heard them called emotional baggage, triggers, and trauma. Whatever you call them, we all have them. Not the same kind, size, or color, but they are there just the same.

We need to recognize that we carry baggage with us wherever we go, and a person may unwittingly trip over it and cause our emotions to flare for an unwanted and unexpected response. This is not that person's fault, they did not know the baggage was there.

After working in a toxic environment where I learned to expect a negative consequence because of a mistake or failure, I no longer felt safe failing. The anticipation of the consequences, even if they were only in my imagination, made my stomach churn, acid crawl up my throat, and sleep elude me.

My past baggage taught me to expect the worst. So, when I had an issue at a new company, I expected to be, at best, scolded and, at worst, fired. I had to coach myself to realize that I am in different circumstances now, and I too have grown.

I am not the same person that packed the baggage in the first place.

When you make a mistake or fail:

- Take ownership. You made the mistake. You failed. Own it.
- Study it. What went wrong? Could it have been avoided?
- Solve it. Fix the mistake. Apologize if you need to.
- Learn from it.

You do not have to berate yourself over a mistake. You do not have to rehash a mistake repeatedly in your head.

When I was first employed and I made an error, I would say, "I wasn't wrong, I was misinformed."

The truth is:

- I was wrong. I know that now, even if I was misinformed. I made a mistake. I needed to take responsibility for my conduct.
- And, I should have apologized to whoever the error affected. It was, after all, an error.

Sometimes, arrogance gets in the way of learning. Just because you were wrong or you made a mistake, does not mean you aren't smart, talented, or an expert. It just means you made an error.

To heal, we need to recognize that no one is perfect. We need to forgive ourselves and others, and we need to get our head on straight. This goes back to knowing:

- Who we are.
- What we want.
- What our purpose is.
- And what is expected.

By knowing these things, you can begin to reset your way of thinking, and your reactions to the world around you and those that inhabit it.

A tool I use for this is called reframing. Reframing is where you turn a negative statement into a positive statement. It is about seeing the world through a lens of positive intention.

Let's try a few exercises:

Negative Statement	Positive Statement
• I don't want to get out of bed.	• I am blessed to have things to do.
• I don't want to go to work.	• I get to go to work.
• I hate pulling weeds.	• I get to spend time outside in my yard.
• Meetings are a waste of time.	• Meetings help us be on the same page.

Reframing is a wonderful way to practice positivity and to see things in another light. It is a tool that helps you heal by releasing negative self-talk and replacing it with upbeat and positive phrases, which are still true.

Healing takes time. It happens on its own schedule. It could take a few hours or a few years. And, when you think the wounds are fully healed something will make them open again. Know that is perfectly normal.

Do not let emotional baggage or old wounds prevent you from being who you are meant to be.

When I was in college, I accepted a manager role for a retail computer company. We sold desktop computers, laptops, software and accessories, and repaired computer hardware. I worked in the store for three years as a sales associate. When my manager quit, and the opportunity to lead the store occurred, I chose to put a pause on my college degree and took the full-time role.

I was excited to grow the business and serve my community in the technology space. Our store was the furthest branch from the company headquarters, so I often traveled to a neighboring city for manager meetings. During these meetings, I learned that the challenges my location was having were not unique. This led me to take the initiative in documenting both the challenges and potential solutions. I then scheduled a meeting with my management team, who were the top executives of the company.

When the meeting took place, before I could really get started the Chief Executive Officer (CEO) told me that none of what I documented was true. He would not even hear me out. The Chief Operating Officer (COO) listened to me at least, and when she tried to provide input on my recommendations, he would cut her off.

My time had been wasted. The issues, which were clearly there and at all locations, did not exist according to the CEO and he would not acknowledge them, even if the COO was willing to talk through them.

I realized that pausing my college degree for an organization that did not care about the issues it had was not worth it. I left the company and went back to school. This experience though, as negative as it was, left a sour taste for management in my mouth that lasted many years. Not only did I not want to be a manager, but I did not want to go above and beyond unless I had buy-in to do so first.

I had to heal from the experience. I had to recognize that the CEO's behavior and his actions were his, and not necessarily a reflection of me or the work I did. I had to understand that not everyone appreciates forward-thinking, problem-solving, or initiative. I had to learn about building buy-in for an idea before running with it.

All of these are lessons.

Did I fail? Yes. Did it prevent me from moving on? No, though it did take time for me to let go of the baggage that the experience gave me.

Healing is a process that lets your light shine. It might flicker in and out to start, but eventually, it will shine with bold bright intensity.

Flash Points:

✦ Nobody is perfect. It is important to give yourself grace and forgiveness.

✦ To heal, you must forgive.

✦ In life, our wounds are not always visible. They are baggage that we carry with us.

✦ Own your mistakes. Study them. Solve them. Learn from them.

✦ Arrogance gets in the way of learning.

✦ Reframing is turning a negative statement into a positive statement, seeing the world through a lens of positivity.

And the peace of God, which passeth all understanding, shall keep your hearts and minds through Christ Jesus.

Bible, King James Version - Philippians 4:7

Chapter 12
Thriving

There is now no condemnation to them which are in Christ Jesus, who walk not after the flesh, but after the Spirit.

Bible, King James Version - Romans 8:1

Living boldly, as your whole authentic self, takes intentionality and courage. When you wake up in the morning, you must choose to be you. That means, you are intentionally thinking, dressing, eating, and working as who you choose to be.

It takes courage because the world would rather we conform than be ourselves. It will grind the edges of your bright star down until you are little more than a round stone if you let it.

Thriving is living as who you are meant to be, working toward and achieving your goals, with forgiveness and love – for yourself and others.

It is not easy. **Choosing and being intentional, consistently day-in and day-out, takes patience and practice until it becomes a habit.**

1. Be intentional about who you are, where you spend your time, and what fills your jar. Are you in balance?

2. Live your purpose. Whatever your purpose is, connect it to what you do for a living, and how you engage with yourself and others.

3. Shout out your big hairy audacious goal – your dream. Hold yourself accountable for making progress on the goals you have set that will allow you to achieve your dream.

4. Understand that you will encounter roadblocks, dead ends, and even fall in a few holes. It isn't how many times you have to turn around, back up, or climb out. It is about giving yourself grace when it happens and continuing to move forward despite the obstacles.

5. Uncommunicated expectations are the recipe for failure. To succeed, we must know what success looks like. If we cannot describe in detail what success looks like, no one will achieve it.

6. Understand that reality is not constant, though we like to pretend that it is. Reality is a construct. Your reality and mine will be different. Accept it and know that the only person you have control over is you.

7. Networking is necessary. It's like when you were a child and would go up to any random kid and ask them to play. It should not be scary. If it is, remember that people like to talk about themselves. Start with questions about the person you are meeting and learn to listen well.

8. Though uncomfortable, it is not bragging to share your successes in life. If we do not tell people what we are good at, then how will they ever know we are a resource? If no one knows you can bake, no one will ever hire you or ask you for a cake.

9. Emotions can be challenging especially when they come wrapped in feedback, constructive or not. You do not have to accept someone else's emotions, or someone else's opinion. They belong to them. You can take the feedback without accepting the emotion or psychological beating they intend.

10. We all feel like imposters. We are all continuously learning. Just because someone else knows more than us about something, does not make us an imposter. It makes us human.

11. Faking it until you make it does not mean lying on your resume. It means that you model those who you want to be like. You take their example and apply it to yourself, until the skills and habits become your own.

12. Everything ends. Recognize when it is time to move on. This sounds simple. It is not. Endings hurt. But we cannot have a beginning unless we have an ending.

13. Forgive, let go of the pain and heal. Reframe negative talk, to yourself or others, into positive statements and let yourself be happy.

14. Understand that everyone has emotional baggage, you just can't see it. Give grace and practice empathy. If someone accidentally stumbles over your baggage, or you trip over someone else's, remember that the reaction you, or they, have has little to do with the current event.

15. Fear is a thief. It steals our joy, our potential, and our peace.

Your light is not meant to be hidden. It is meant to be shared. **You may be a beacon that inspires others; a guide that illuminates the way; or a comforting glow that dispels the darkness.**

When you sparkle, shine for the world to see, loudly and without reservation.

Thrive.

No man, when he hath lighted a candle, putteth it in a secret place, neither under a bushel, but on a candlestick, that they which come in may see the light.

Bible, King James Version - Luke 11:33

Epilogue

Then shall thy light break forth as the morning, and thine health shall spring forth speedily: and thy righteousness shall go before thee; the glory of the LORD shall be thy reward.

Bible, King James Version - Isaiah 58:8:

Rarely are we constantly shining. Our light fades in and out, may twinkle like the stars, or shimmer like Christmas lights. Some lights are cool, their crisp white light a beacon. Others are warm and inviting, their yellow light a wavering flicker. And some are bonfires that we gather around.

I hope that through these pages you connected with who you really are, what you really want, and that you know what path you are illuminating with your light.

You are unique. You are fearfully and wonderfully made. There is no other light in this universe, or other universes, which is the same as yours.

I shared with you that I declare Jesus Christ as my Lord and Savior. My faith, my belief, and my love are core components of who I am. All I do glorifies Him. Thank you for the opportunity to share my experiences and the tidbits of wisdom I have gleaned or that have been shared with me over the years.

The next few paragraphs and pages share my testimony.

I have always felt connected to the spiritual. It began when I was an infant. If you remember from the second chapter, I experienced second- and third-degree burns when I was eight months old.

When the accident occurred, I was sent to the hospital for two weeks. I could not voice my pain with words, so I screamed and cried. My mom prayed over me, and she said she felt a presence enter the room. I calmed, then quieted. The expression on my face was one of peace, not pain.

I do not remember this time, but I like the story.

As a child, I grew up culturally Lutheran, which is a Christian denomination. That means I was baptized as an infant in a Lutheran church and was raised with Lutheran beliefs.

There was a picture of Jesus hanging in my bedroom, with Him poised to knock on a door. I was taught to pray and talk with God every night. And, though I did not spend much time in a church building, I was protected and watched over. I felt God in my life.

Even with this connection to God, there was a lot of spiritual activity around me. Throughout my life, I heard, saw, and felt a lot of spiritual noise. Images, creatures, hauntings, and more were normal for me. (It is okay if you think me delusional. Many people, even Christians, do not understand the Spiritual.)

In college, I started seeking to understand Christianity. I took a course in Religious Studies, which is great to learn about world religions at the highest level possible but not good for learning about the Christian God and Jesus Christ. I started attending church with my boyfriend and attending Bible studies. And I started reading the Bible.

My boyfriend had a revelation and accepted Jesus Christ as his Lord and Savior and was baptized. Through his baptism and the study of baptism, I began to believe that sprinkling me with water as an infant was not what God intended. It seemed to me to be more of a promise to God to raise me to know Him, but that baptism should be my decision.

I was then convicted to be baptized. It was difficult telling my parents. They did not understand why I would want to be baptized when I had already been baptized. That is because they believed in the tenets of the Lutheran faith. I no longer did. I believed that after professing Jesus Christ as my Lord and Savior that I should be baptized, which meant fully immersed in water.

So, I was.

It was a transformational experience. When I came out of the water, the world was silent. Completely, totally silent. Never in my life had it been silent before. I could no longer feel or hear the spiritual realm.

Everyone's salvation story is different. They are each unique. All you have to do is accept and profess Jesus Christ as your Lord and Savior. That is it.

For the first part of my life, I always felt connected with God, but I did not know God. I did not have a relationship or understanding of Him. Building a relationship with Him means spending time reading the scriptures, praying, and talking to Him every day and any time, worshipping Him, and fellowshipping with Believers. It means steadfastly keeping your faith.

God is love. He wants us to live boldly, joyfully, and without worries.

For God, who commanded the light to shine out of darkness, hath shined in our hearts, to give the light of the knowledge of the glory of God in the face of Jesus Christ.

Bible, King James Version, 2 Corinthians 4:6

The Bible is a book about God. It lets us get to know Him, helps us to understand Him, and instructs us on how He wants us to live. Every time you read it, you will have a new or deeper understanding.

God does not want us changing His scriptures. What is there is what is there. It is not about interpreting it through current cultural norms or dismissing pieces of it because "that was just the times."

And God is not about us passing judgement on each other. Judgement is reserved for Him. So, love the person, not the sin. Pray for Bob at work, who sabotages your project or Tina who belittles you so that she looks better. God asks us to love our enemies, which means to treat them just like our neighbors who we love as ourselves.

Being in a relationship with God does not mean your life gets easier, it means that you know in the end who wins.

Whatever your light, I hope through this journey of Sparkling Lights that you have found a spark of passion, a ray of insight, a lightning bolt of hope, or a rainbow of truth.

But the path of the just is as the shining light, that shineth more and more unto the perfect day.

Bible, King James Version, Proverbs 4:18

Notes

✦ Sparkling Lights ✦

About the Author

Depending on the day, **AD Krasikov** may be outgoing or reserved, flamboyant or traditional, a chatterbox or quiet. She is an observer, a storyteller, a strategist. It is her purpose in life to make a difference.

Raised by an engineer and a serial entrepreneur, she learned from an early age to use facts when making a request, and that failure is only a setback towards success.

She is ever curious and built a lengthy career in financial services, moving from Information Technology to Business Analysis, and then to Project Management where she had an opportunity to learn about and explore many facets of the industry.

This led AD to Product Management and E-Commerce. From there to Digital Marketing, Marketing Research, and Marketing Communications. Next, came operationalizing a customer relationship management solution and managing organizational change, followed by Payments, Digital Experience, and Executive Leadership.

AD graduated from the University of Colorado at Colorado Springs magna cum laude with a Bachelor of Arts degree in Cultural Anthropology and a minor in Organizational Management. She is a certified Credit Union Development Educator, a certified Strategic Marketing Executive, and a certified Agile Product Manager.

AD is a speaker, author, and mentor. She is passionate about humans – each individual person – and strives to make a difference, as best she can, in the lives she touches.

An avid reader, she enjoys a wide array of genres and admits to an addiction to original voiceover, subtitled, foreign dramas.

www.ingramcontent.com/pod-product-compliance
Lightning Source LLC
Chambersburg PA
CBHW060408050426
42449CB00009B/1937